VASCO NÚÑEZ DE BALBOA

Kristin Petrie

Checkerboard Library

An Imprint of Abdo Publishing
abdobooks.com

ABDOBOOKS.COM

Published by Abdo Publishing, a division of ABDO, PO Box 398166, Minneapolis, Minnesota 55439.
Copyright © 2022 by Abdo Consulting Group, Inc. International copyrights reserved in all countries.
No part of this book may be reproduced in any form without written permission from the publisher.
Checkerboard Library™ is a trademark and logo of Abdo Publishing.

Printed in the United States of America, North Mankato, Minnesota
102021
012022

Design and Production: Tamara JM Peterson, Mighty Media, Inc.
Editor: Liz Salzmann
Cover Photograph: Wikimedia Commons
Interior Photographs: Amable-Paul Coutan/Wikimedia Commons, p. 15; Ayaita/Wikimedia Commons, pp. 16–17; Galina Savina/Shutterstock Images, p. 27; Irina Kovancova/Shutterstock Images, p. 13; Jazzmany/Shutterstock Images, pp. 9, 28 (top); Kean Collection/Getty Images, p. 23; Michael Sittow/Wikimedia Commons, pp. 19, 29 (bottom); MicroOne/Shutterstock Images, pp. 20–21, 21 (inset map); Preto Perola/Shutterstock Images, pp. 10–11, 28 (bottom right); Travel reports/Shutterstock Images, pp. 6–7; Wikimedia Commons, pp. 5, 8, 28 (bottom left); ZU_09/iStockphoto, pp. 25, 29 (top)
Design Elements: Joseph Moxon/Flickr (map), Oleg Iatsun/Shutterstock Images (compass rose)

Library of Congress Control Number: 2021943039

Publisher's Cataloging-in-Publication Data
Names: Petrie, Kristin, author.
Title: Vasco Núñez de Balboa / by Kristin Petrie
Description: Minneapolis, Minnesota : Abdo Publishing, 2022 | Series: World explorers | Includes online resources and index.
Identifiers: ISBN 9781532197291 (lib. bdg.) | ISBN 9781098219420 (ebook)
Subjects: LCSH: Balboa, Vasco Núñez de, 1475-1519--Juvenile literature. | Discovery and exploration--Juvenile literature. | Exploring expeditions--Juvenile literature. | Explorers--Biography--Juvenile literature.
Classification: DDC 970.01--dc23

CONTENTS

VASCO NÚÑEZ DE BALBOA 4

GROWING UP 6

EARLY TRAVELS 8

THE NEW WORLD 10

FARMER 12

SOUTH AMERICA 14

DARIÉN 16

GOVERNOR BALBOA 18

EXPEDITIONS 22

THE PACIFIC OCEAN 24

THE ADVENTURE ENDS 26

TIMELINE 28

GLOSSARY 30

SAYING IT 31

ONLINE RESOURCES 31

INDEX 32

VASCO NÚÑEZ DE BALBOA

In 1513, Spanish explorer Vasco Núñez de Balboa became the first European to see the Pacific Ocean. Balboa's journey to the Pacific was filled with hardship and loss. He faced these things in the hope of finding adventure. But he was also consumed with greed.

Many Europeans crossed the Atlantic Ocean in search of fame and wealth. They often accomplished their goals by overthrowing Native American peoples. Then, they claimed the lands and resources for their own countries. Balboa followed the examples set by his fellow explorers. Throughout the centuries, exploration by Balboa and others has increased our knowledge of the world.

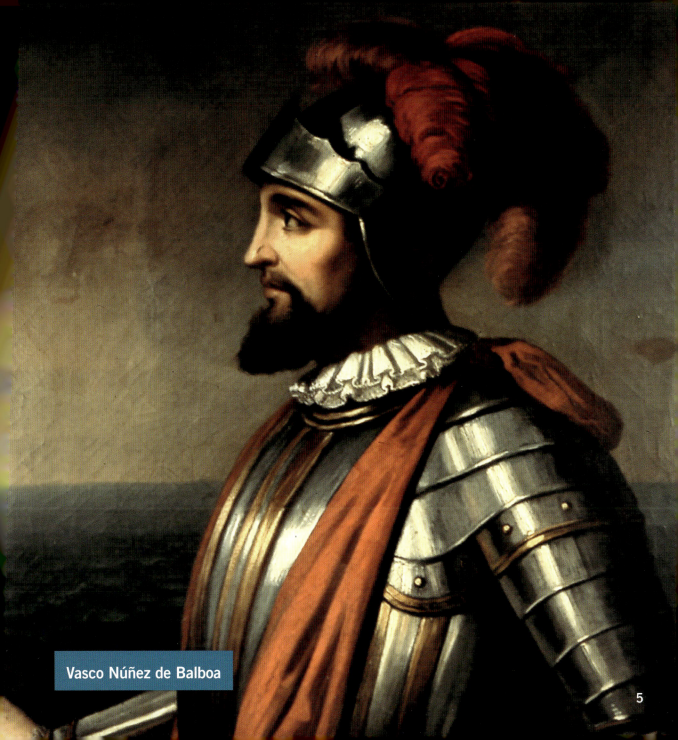
Vasco Núñez de Balboa

GROWING UP

Vasco Núñez de Balboa was born around 1475 in Jerez de los Caballeros, Spain. This town was in the Badajoz **province** on Spain's southwest coast, near the border of Portugal. Little is known about Vasco's family. Nothing is known about his mother. His father was a poor nobleman.

At that time, a boy of noble birth usually left his home to begin training as a knight. So, Vasco was sent to Moguer, Spain. There, Vasco served as a **page** to the Lord of Moguer. In exchange for his work, Vasco learned to hunt, play music, and dance. He also received military training.

During Vasco's time in Moguer, important events took place in Europe. Ships were improved so they could sail longer and farther. Explorers searched for unknown lands and new sea routes to the Indies, or southeast Asia. This is where valuable trading took place.

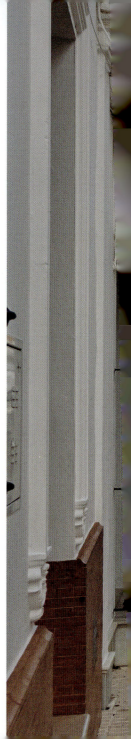

Moguer is located near the west coast of Spain.

EARLY TRAVELS

One explorer made big news. Christopher Columbus claimed to have found a western sea route to Asia in 1492. In reality, he had sailed to islands in the Caribbean Sea. Still, Europeans realized Columbus had found a new treasure, the Americas.

After following Columbus's route, other explorers returned to Moguer. They shared exciting stories about the New World. In 1500, Balboa got his chance to sail to the New World. A wealthy man named Rodrigo de Bastidas planned an expedition to cross the Atlantic Ocean.

Balboa eagerly boarded one of Bastidas's ships. Balboa was 25 years old. When the ships left Spain, it was the last time Balboa saw his **homeland**.

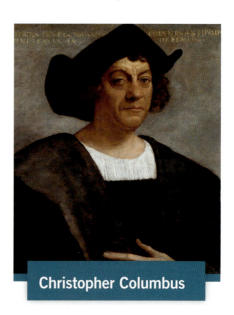

Christopher Columbus

WOULD YOU?

Would you find it hard to leave behind your home and everything familiar? Do you think Balboa was able to take anything with him?

There is a statue of Rodrigo de Bastidas in Santa Marta, Colombia.

THE NEW WORLD

Bastidas's ships crossed the Atlantic Ocean. After reaching South America, most **fleets** sailed down the east coast. But Bastidas decided to follow the north coast.

The small expedition explored the coast of present-day Colombia. The ships continued west. They reached the Gulf of Urabá, near the **Isthmus** of Panama. Balboa noted a Native American settlement on Panama's mainland. The people there were friendly. But Bastidas's expedition had too few men to establish a settlement. So, in 1502, they sailed on to the island of Hispaniola.

Hispaniola was the site of Columbus's first Spanish settlement. Balboa was happy there. He was not ready to return to Spain. He wanted more adventure.

Today, Hispaniola is divided between two countries. These are the Dominican Republic and Haiti.

FARMER

For seven years, Balboa tried to make a living on Hispaniola as a farmer. But farming did not bring him the wealth and glory he wanted. In fact, he went deeply into **debt**.

In 1509, an expedition was planned to start a Spanish colony on South America's mainland. Soldiers and sailors lined up to be included. Balboa also applied. However, Balboa was not allowed to join because of his debts. So, the expedition left without him. It established the San Sebastian colony on the coast of the Gulf of Urabá.

The next year, Martín Fernández de Enciso planned an expedition to take supplies and settlers to the new colony. This time, Balboa was determined to go. He wanted adventure and to escape his **creditors**. So, he hid in a large barrel aboard one of the ships. Soon, Balboa was on his way to San Sebastian!

Balboa may not have been the only stowaway. Some say that he hid his dog, Leoncico, in the barrel too!

SOUTH AMERICA

With Balboa hiding on board, Enciso's expedition reached San Sebastian. To the crew's surprise, many of the original colonists had fled the area. The remaining Spaniards were desperate for help.

Francisco Pizarro was the leader of the surviving Spaniards. He said that they had trouble getting enough food. Also, the Native American people were hostile toward the Spaniards. They often attacked them. The Spaniards needed a plan.

By this time, Balboa had become a member of Enciso's crew. He suggested that they move across the Gulf of Urabá to the town of Darién.

WOULD YOU?

Would you have been brave enough to suggest moving to a new town? Do you think Balboa was nervous about being responsible for all of the men?

Francisco Pizarro

DARIÉN

Darién was the Native American settlement Balboa had seen when he first arrived in the New World. He knew that the people there were more welcoming. He also remembered that they grew food. So, the men agreed to move to the west side of the gulf.

At Darién, the colonists and Enciso's crew found that Balboa was right. There was plenty of food. They also found cotton and other treasures. And the Spaniards soon secured gold by either trading with or fighting the Native Americans.

The Spaniards established a colony at Darién. They called it Santa María la Antigua del Darién. Then, Balboa made plans to take over the colony.

Today, one of the most common Native American groups in the Darién area is the Chocó.

GOVERNOR BALBOA

As the expedition leader, Enciso thought he should rule the new colony. But Balboa wanted the power. So, he convinced the Spaniards to remove Enciso from leadership. Enciso was furious, so he returned to Spain to seek King Ferdinand II's help.

After Enciso left, a newly appointed governor named Diego de Nicuesa arrived to solve the leadership problem. Balboa used his influence to turn the Spaniards against Nicuesa as well.

The colonists needed a new leader. So, they elected Balboa and a man named Zamudio to rule the colony. But Balboa didn't want to share the power. So, he convinced Zamudio to return to Spain with gold. Finally in December 1511, King Ferdinand named Balboa temporary governor of Darién.

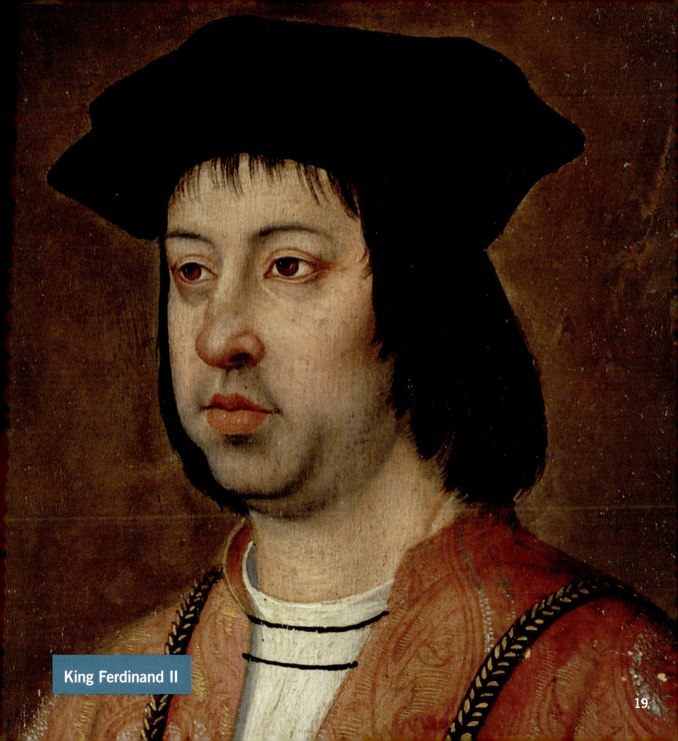

King Ferdinand II

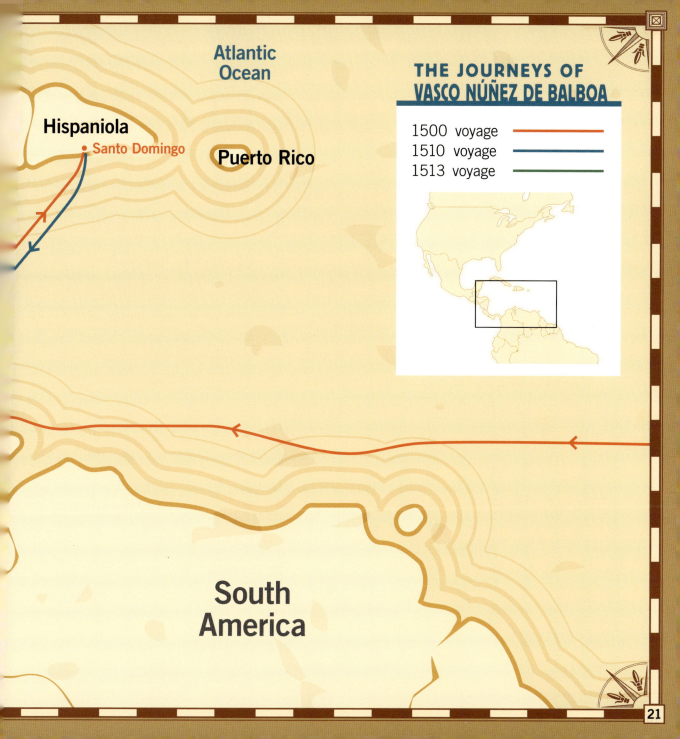

EXPEDITIONS

Balboa enjoyed being governor of Darién. He had both wealth and power. Nevertheless, he was restless. He wanted adventure. Balboa was sure there was more gold and glory to be found in the New World.

Balboa began leading expeditions from Darién into Panama. He tried first to become **allies** with the Native American people he met. But some did not want to give up their ways of life or be under Spain's rule. In those cases, Balboa conquered them.

WOULD YOU?

Would you have believed tales of a great sea or a land of gold? Would you have risked everything to go in search of these places?

Balboa heard tales of a great sea from many Native Americans. They said the sea lay on the other side of the mountains. And, the Native Americans spoke of a wealthy nation farther south. They were referring to the Pacific Ocean and Peru. Balboa was determined to see these places.

Balboa talking to Native Americans in Panama

THE PACIFIC OCEAN

On September 1, 1513, Balboa began his search for the great sea and the wealthy nation. His expedition was composed of 190 Spaniards and hundreds of Native Americans. They sailed from Darién and landed near Acla, on Panama's north coast.

From Acla, the troops marched south across Panama for about three weeks. On September 25, one of Balboa's guides pointed to a mountain. The guide told Balboa that the great sea lay just beyond it.

When the expedition was near the top of the mountain, Balboa ordered the men to wait for him there. Balboa continued to the mountain peak alone. He looked down and became the first European to see the Pacific Ocean.

Some days later, Balboa and his men reached the coast of the Gulf of San Miguel. Balboa stood in the shallow water. He raised his sword and claimed the entire sea and nearby lands for Spain.

The Spaniards called the ocean *Mar del Sur*, or "South Sea." Later, it was renamed the Pacific Ocean.

THE ADVENTURE ENDS

Balboa had made a huge claim for his country. But at the same time, King Ferdinand sent Pedro Arias Dávila, usually called Pedrarias, to take over as governor of Darién. Rumors started by rivals such as Enciso had given Balboa a bad reputation in Spain.

Reports of Balboa's discoveries eventually reached Spain. These reports repaired Balboa's reputation. King Ferdinand named him **adelantado** of the *Mar del Sur*, or "South Sea," and governor of the Panama and Coiba **provinces**. While serving as governor, Balboa continued to explore the Gulf of San Miguel.

Meanwhile, Pedrarias was jealous of the successful and adventurous Balboa. In 1518, Pedrarias falsely charged Balboa of treason. Balboa was tried and **sentenced** to death. On January 12, 1519, Vasco Núñez de Balboa was **beheaded**.

Today, Balboa is remembered for his many accomplishments. One unit of money in Panama is called a "Balboa." There is also a town in Panama named after him.

Today, the Panama Canal crosses Panama. It allows ships to sail between the Atlantic and Pacific Oceans.

27

TIMELINE

1500

Balboa joins Rodrigo de Bastidas's expedition to South America.

1475

Vasco Núñez de Balboa is born in Jerez de los Caballeros, Spain.

1502

Balboa becomes a farmer on Hispaniola.

1510
Balboa stows away on Enciso's expedition to South America.

1513
Balboa becomes the first European to see the Pacific Ocean.

1511
King Ferdinand names Balboa temporary governor of Darién.

1519
On January 12, Balboa is beheaded for treason.

GLOSSARY

adelantado—a military title given to some Spanish conquistadors during the 1400s to 1600s.

allies—people or countries that agree to help each other in times of need.

behead—to cut off the head of someone, especially as a punishment.

creditor—a person or a company that is owed money or goods.

debt—something owed to someone, usually money.

fleet—a group of ships under one command.

homeland—the country where someone was born or grew up.

isthmus—a narrow strip of land connecting two larger land areas.

page—a boy being trained to be a knight in the Middle Ages.

province—a geographical or governmental division of a country.

sentenced—given a punishment for a crime.

SAYING IT

Badajoz—bah-dah-HOHTH

Darién—dahr-YEHN

Hispaniola—hihs-puhn-YOH-luh

isthmus—IHS-muhs

Jerez de los Caballeros—hay-REHTH day lohs kah-bah-YAY-rohs

Moguer—moh-GEHR

Rodrigo de Bastidas—roh-DREE-goh day bahs-TEE-dahs

ONLINE RESOURCES

To learn more about Vasco Núñez de Balboa, please visit **abdobooklinks.com** or scan this QR code. These links are routinely monitored and updated to provide the most current information available.

INDEX

Asia, 6, 8
Atlantic Ocean, 4, 8, 10

Bastidas, Rodrigo de, 8, 10
birth, 6

Caribbean Sea, 8
childhood, 6
Coiba, 26
Colombia, 10
colonization, 12, 14, 16, 18
Columbus, Christopher, 8, 10

Darién, 10, 14, 16, 18, 22, 24, 26
Dávila, Pedro Arias "Pedrarias," 26
death, 26

Enciso, Martín Fernández de, 12, 14, 16, 18, 26
Europe, 4, 6, 8, 24

family, 6
farming, 12
Ferdinand II (king of Spain), 18, 26

Gulf of San Miguel, 24, 26
Gulf of Urabá, 10, 12, 14

Hispaniola, 10, 12

Mar del Sur, 26

Native Americans, 4, 10, 14, 16, 22, 24
New World, 8, 10, 12, 16, 22
Nicuesa, Diego de, 18

Pacific Ocean, 4, 22, 24
Panama, 10, 22, 24, 26
Peru, 22
Pizarro, Francisco, 14
Portugal, 6

San Sebastian, 12, 14
South America, 10, 12
Spain, 4, 6, 8, 10, 12, 14, 16, 18, 22, 24, 26

trading, 6, 16
treasure, 8, 16

wealth, 4, 8, 12, 22, 24

Zamudio, 18